POSITIVE
PRAYERS
FOR
POWER-FILLED
LIVING

POSITIVE PRAYERS FOR POWER-FILLED LIVING

Robert H. Schuller

HAWTHORN BOOKS, INC.
W. Clement Stone, Publisher
New York

And whatever you ask in prayer
you will receive if you have faith.

Matt. 21:22

Contents

Acknowledgments

I wish to acknowledge my thanks to the thousands of friends and fellow church members who have been a source of inspiration to me during my public ministry. This collection of prayers is being published on the twenty-fifth anniversary of my ordination. During these twenty-five years, I have published nine books and thousands of sermons.

From all of my published writings, I have selected material which has proved to be most helpful for daily living, and I am compiling it in a revised form of prayers. The prayers of Jesus and from the Old Testament are from *The Living Bible Paraphrased*, copyright © 1971 by Tyndale House Publishers, and are used by permission of the publisher. The prayer by E. Stanley Jones is quoted from *The Way* by E. Stanley Jones and used by permission of the publisher, Abingdon Press, Nashville.

My special thanks to my wife, Arvella Schuller, who assisted in compiling and editing this material, and my secretary, Tracy Hartman, and her assistant, Joan Gore, for their assistance in preparing my manuscript.

PRINCIPLES
OF
PRAYER

What Is Prayer?

The greatest power in the world today is the power of people to communicate with Almighty God.

Prayer is not a scheme whereby we can move God into our lives but rather a spiritual exercise through which we draw ourselves toward God until we are a part of his plan and his purpose.

The purpose of prayer is not to give you what you want when you want it but to make you the kind of person God wanted you to be when he put you on the planet Earth.

Six Steps to Prayer

Pursue God—

Begin by confession of sin, be specific, use harsh, embarrassing words that bluntly describe you as you are. "If with all your heart you truly seek him, you shall surely find him . . ."
(Deut. 4:29)

Re-examine yourself—

Ask yourself, "Am I sincerely honest?" Play no games! Make no pretenses! If your problem is doubt, then admit it. For instance, pray, "I thank you, God, that you love me even when my faith is dim, dark, and dreary."

Affirm positively what God is able to do within you—

In your honesty, do remain affirmative. Negative praying only weakens you. Pray, "I know that you love me anyway. I know that you are waiting eagerly to forgive me for . . ."

Yield your self-will to God—

"Not my will, but yours be done, O God."
(Luke 22:42)

Expect positive results—

Anticipate positive emotions, sense the joy, peace, and faith flowing into you. "If you have faith, all things are possible."
(Matt. 17:30)

Rejoice!—

In thanking God, be specific, detail your thanks. For example, "Thank you, God, for eyes to see the faces of those I love, for ears to hear my favorite music, the sound of a friend's voice on the telephone in the middle of a lonely hour of life."

God Always Answers Prayer

When the idea is not right, God says, "No."
No—when the idea is not the best.
No—when the idea is absolutely wrong.
No—when though it may help you, it could create problems for someone else.

When the time is not right, God says, "Slow."
What a catastrophe it would be if God answered every prayer at the snap of your fingers. Do you know what would happen? God would become your servant, not your master. Suddenly God would be working for you instead of you working for God.

Remember: God's delays are not God's denials. God's timing is perfect. Patience is what we need in prayer.

When you are not right, God says, "Grow."
The selfish person has to grow in unselfishness.
The cautious person must grow in courage.
The timid person must grow in confidence.
The dominating person must grow in sensitivity.
The critical person must grow in tolerance.
The negative person must grow in positive attitudes.
The pleasure-seeking person must grow in compassion for suffering people.

When everything is all right, God says, "Go."
Then miracles happen:
A hopeless alcoholic is set free!
A drug addict finds release!
A doubter becomes as a child in his belief.
Diseased tissue responds to treatment, and healing begins.
The door to your dream suddenly swings open and there stands God saying, "Go!"

THE
PRAYERS

PRAYERS
FOR
DAILY
LIVING

God Loves Me!

Thank you, Lord, for this holy sentence,
this good news,
this happy report,
this exciting thought,
this graceful truth,
this fantastic lesson. God loves me!
Even when I'm at my worst—
God loves me.
Even when my faith is dim—
God loves me anyway!
It's incomprehensible and fantastic!
Thank you, Father.
Amen.

Thank You

Thank you, Lord:
You are the Light that never goes out.
You are the Eye that never closes,
You are the Ear that is never shut,
You are the Mind that never gives up,
You are the Heart that never grows cold, and
You are the Hand that never stops reaching.
Amen.

Faith

Lord, I believe
In the sun, even when
it is behind the clouds;
In the seed, even when
it lies unsprouted under the ground;
In faith, even when I have been
betrayed;
In love, even when I have been
rejected;
In hope, even when I have been
hurt;
In God, even when
you do not answer my prayers.
Amen.

Grow Power

I must be growing,
Lord!

I always used to say: "I've got
to see it before I believe it."

Now I'm affirming: "I've got to
believe it before I see it!"

Keep giving me grow power, Lord.
Amen.

Love Power

Lord!

No problem is too big
for your power.

No person is too small
for your love!

Hallelujah!
Amen.

What a Friend!

You have never failed,
Lord,
to be my one, essential, intimate friend.
When I was:
Lonely in striving—you encouraged me.
Lonely in struggling—you lifted me.
Lonely in serving—you supported me.
Lonely in suffering—you comforted me.
Lonely in sinning—you forgave me.
Lonely in sinking—you renewed me.
Lonely in succeeding—you rejoiced with me.

What a friend I have in Jesus!
Thank you, Lord.
Amen.

Your Plan

I have come to you, Lord,
For a new lift,
A new load,
A new love,
A new light
on my life's road.
I have a powerful, positive
suspicion that you have a plan
for my today and my tomorrow,
and that this beautiful plan
is unfolding exactly
as it should!
I will stop trying
to understand, and instead
start enjoying whatever
comes my way!
Amen.

Positive Thoughts

Thank you, Lord,
for the exciting
ideas you are
waiting to send into
my thinking
mind! I'd explode
with enthusiasm
if I could think of
all the positive thoughts
waiting to come
out of my God-
inspired brain.
Amen.

Bend Me!

Keep me
Soft enough,
Lord,
So you can
Bend me
Into the shape
You want
My life
To take.
Amen.

Love

Love
is my deciding
to make someone else's problem
my problem.

Help me to love
my fellow persons
that way, Lord.
Amen.

I Am Waiting

Thank you, Lord, for your messages
that come from the deepest, unexplored,
unfathomable seas of silence.
Through beautiful, positive thoughts
you come into my mind.
Oh, Lord, it is going to be a great day!
I am waiting. I am ready.
I am listening. I will move.
Amen.

Let Me Dare

Lord,
give me the
courage to
dare to love.
It's risky, I know,
for I might be
rejected, and that hurts.
Or love-starved people
will leap to respond
to this rare
offer of honest affection,
and they may expect
too much—too soon.
So give me the nerve to
live bravely and love
dangerously! I may lose
my freedom, but
at least I won't be lonely.
In the name of my Savior, Jesus Christ.
Amen.

My Walk

O God, I'm inspired.
For you have just impressed
this truth into my mind:
The most powerful force in the world
is a positive idea in the mind of a
believer who is walking in your will!
I now reach forth my life and say,
"God, put my life into the center of
your will."
Amen.

I Respond

Thank you, Lord, for bringing me to the
place where love can knock at the door
of my heart. O Father, do not let
me be afraid. I shall not resist your
affectionate touch. Let me, O Lord,
have the spirit of a little child and
dare to respond and run with open arms to
your call of love.
Amen.

Something Beautiful

Father, I turn these minutes over to you.
Do something beautiful in my mind,
in my heart, and in my life today.
So I will look back and say: "I was
caught up by an inspiring spirit of the
eternal God in this moment of prayer."
In the name of Christ I pray.
Amen.

This Moment

Father,
I have a strong sensation
that
you brought me to this moment of prayer
because
you plan to share with me
insights to solve my problems.

So I will go out
and
face the sunlight of a new day
and a new week
crammed with undiscovered possibilities.
I am encouraged!
I am enthused!
I am more hopeful than I have been in a long time!
Amen.

Beauty

Thank you, Father, for filling the world
with beauty.
I thank you for the beauty of life,
the beauty of love,
the beauty of children, and
the beauty of old people.
I thank you for the
beauty of Christ and for the beauty of
any life when Christ is invited through
the Holy Spirit. Thank you, Father,
that you have made my life beautiful too.
Amen.

Sunshine

Like a fresh
burst of golden sunshine that
dissolves the gloomy fog
and makes the glistening grass
sparkle with a green sheen,
so, Lord, you have come
into my mind
at the opening of a new day
assuring me that life is going
to be beautiful.
It's going to be one of my
great days—after all!
Amen.

I'll Try!

Lord,

I'd rather attempt to do something great
and fail,

Than attempt to do nothing and succeed!

I'll try—with your help!
Amen.

Great Goals

Lord,

Thank you
For great goals!

Let them be my uplifting aims.
But
never let my targets
become ceilings!

Amen.

Possibilities
Unlimited

I can count
the seeds in an apple.
But, Lord—you alone
can count the apples
in one seed!

Some things are
impossible,Lord!
It's impossible for me
to see the immeasurable, unlimited
possibilities in one
fertile idea.
Praise the Lord.
Amen.

Success

As I become
a success
with your help,
Lord,
let me never forget
that
what I am
is more important
than what I do.
Faith stimulates success.
Hope sustains success.
Love sanctifies success.
So I cannot
and I dare not
succeed without your
power, peace, and pressure
in my life,
Jesus Christ.
Amen.

New Problems

Thank you for the success I am enjoying,
Lord.

Even though
I've just come to realize
that
when we succeed we don't eliminate problems:
We exchange our present problems
for bigger ones! But
great things happen
when "possibility thinkers" run into
mountains!

I'm holding on to you, Lord!
Amen.

Do Something

It's better
to do something imperfectly
than
to do nothing perfectly.

Lord, help me to
overcome my unrealistic perfectionism
without forfeiting my pursuit for excellence.
Amen.

"Possibility Thinkers"

Lord, when I face a mountain,
do not let me quit!
Give me the strength to keep on striving
until I climb over,
find a pass through,
or tunnel underneath.
And if my best efforts fail,
give me the patience to stay
and the perception to see
the possibilities
of turning my mountain into a goldmine
with your help.
Amen.

Surprises

Thank you, Father, for the beautiful
surprises you are planning for me today.
So often in my life, when it looked like
the day would be dismal, depressing, and
dark, an unexpected burst of golden
sunshine exploded through a black cloud
sending inspiring shafts of warm,
beautiful sunshine into my life.
Father, it is happening now!
I can already feel the power of
your love, through Christ my Lord.
Amen.

Change

People
who never change their minds
are either perfect to begin with
or stubborn forever after.

So I'm willing, wanting, and waiting
to change into the person
you want me to be, Lord.
Amen.

Fill Me!

O Lord, like the thirsty deer which goes
to drink from the mountain spring;
like the growing flower which turns hungrily
to the satisfying sun;
like the empty pitcher which is carried to the
fountain to be filled;
so I come, O God, knowing
that in this time of prayer
my soul will be filled
with your love and your truth.
Thank you!
Amen.

People

Lord, there are some people who, when
I am around them, fatigue me.
And there are other people who,
surrounding me, energize me.
Jesus, you are that exciting
kind of person! I draw so much
energy-producing enthusiasm
for living when I allow your spirit
to fill my life.
Amen.

I Am Eager!

Lord, you've put the whole world
together and you've put me in the
middle of it because you want to say
something to me and through me today.
May your beautiful peace fall gently,
softly, sweetly, and beautifully
upon my mind—now.
I am ready to listen and eager to move
ahead, today, with "possibility thinking."
Amen.

Christ-Filled Life

Any person's life
is found to
change for the
better when Christ
is invited in!
Come, Lord,
into my life—now.
Amen.

I'm Ready

Lord,
I'm ready to
Become a Christian.
Not because
I'm against something
But because
I'm in love with someone.
I love you, Jesus Christ!
Amen.

Make Me a Christian

Holy Spirit, fill my life by
making me a true Christ-In.
A mind through which Christ thinks,
A heart through which Christ loves,
A tongue through which Christ speaks,
A face through which Christ glows,
A hand through which Christ lifts.
Amen.

Cleanse Me

God, I have not been living according
to your will. I have only been doing
what I want to do. I have been sinning.
I have been disobedient. I give you
now the areas of my life that need to be
cleansed. Jesus Christ, save me.
Amen.

I Want to Improve

O God, how thankful I am that you have come
into my life through the Holy Spirit.
I'm willing to say: "I'm not perfect, Lord!
I want to improve. Show me where I can."
So, Father, I sense that a miracle is
happening in my life right now.
You are doing something beautiful in
my heart this very moment.
I thank and praise you!
Amen.

To Share My Faith

Lord, show me the person
you want to speak to
through my life
today.
Amen.

No Gain
Without Pain

You reminded
me again, today,
Lord.
There is no gain
without pain.
I must be
making headway
because I hurt.
Hallelujah!
Amen.

Together

Thank you, God!

For mountains
that will turn
into miracles!

I'll keep the faith:
you give the power.
Together we'll win.
Amen.

PRAYERS
FOR
SPECIAL TIMES
AND
EVENTS

At Dawn

At the beginning of a new day,
Lord,
I sit in a choice seat.
I wait expectantly
for the curtain to go up
and
for the drama to begin.

I will see faces of people today, Lord,
and I will see your love in their life!

Truly, Lord,
at the end of this day,
I will have been deeply touched.
I will have been greatly moved
for I will have seen proof
of the reality of the love of God
in a human life.
Amen.

Marriage

O God, look down upon us as we begin
our married life on our knees. Jesus
Christ, we pray that your Holy Spirit
will come to make our hearts your home.
So may you be the head of our house.
May you be the unseen guest at every
meal.
The silent listener to every word that
is spoken.
The friend that never slumbers or sleeps.
The one who can bring peace in times of
tension and restore joy after sorrow.
Father, our path may take us through
difficult years ahead.
So be with us through our laughter and tears,
through our labor and leisure, through our
lying down and our rising up.
Always remind us that our Lord is forever
within our reach, keeping watch over his own.
You have brought us together, a young man
and a young woman to become one in marriage.
O God, our life's plan is unfolding as it
should. Now we stand, hand in hand,
husband and wife. This is our golden moment,
our happy hour.
May all the love we hope for and all the
joy we pray for come true. And may our
highest expectations be realized and our
most beautiful dreams find full blossom
in the years that are ahead. This is our
prayer. In the name of Christ our Savior,
we pray!
Amen.

A Parent's Prayer

I believe, O Lord, that my children are
a gift of God! The hope of a new tomorrow.
I thank you for the immeasurable
possibilities that lie slumbering in each
son and daughter.
I thank you that you have designed a
perfect plan for their future, and that
your love shall always surround them.
I trust you to help them to grow up—
first creeping, then toddling, then
standing, stretching skyward for a decade
and a half until they reach full
stature—a man—a woman!
I believe that they can, and will, be
molded and shaped between infancy and
adulthood—as a tree is shaped by the
gardener, as the clay vessel is molded
in the potter's hand, as the shoreline of
the sea is carved under the patient hand
of the endless waves—by home and church,
by school and street, through sights and
sounds, the touch of my hand on their life,
and Christ's spirit in their heart!
I believe that they shall mature as only
people can—through laughter and tears,
through trial and error, by reward and
punishment, through affection and
discipline, until they stretch their wings
and leave the nest to fly!
O God, I believe in my children.
Help me so to live that they may always
have good reasons to believe in me—
and so in thee.
Amen.

Children's Morning Prayers

Good morning, God! I am so glad that
you are my friend. Together we make a
great team. I am not afraid of anything
when you are beside me. It will be a
good day if you will think through my
brain, talk through my tongue, and
smile at people through my face. In my
work or play, may my friends and even strangers
see that I love you.
Amen.

Good morning, God! Thank you for your
beautiful world! I want to make your
world even more beautiful. So may my
face be like happy sunshine and not a dark
cloud.
Amen.

A Child's Evening Prayer

Dear Lord, hear my evening prayer.
Thank you for your loving care.
Bless all those I love tonight,
Keep us safe till morning light.
Teach me to love in work and play,
Make tomorrow a wonderful day.
Forgive me when I do things wrong.
You're my special friend my whole
life long.
Amen.

Independence Day

We come, a happy crowd of fun-loving people, held captive
by a deep belief in human freedom, celebrating today our
joys in this free land.

Tonight, when explosions of light illuminate with color the
black sky, may our imaginations burst with a new inspiration, dreaming of that beautiful day when the bright sparks
of refreshing freedom will shower upon the parched nations
of the world where oppressed people thirst for the freedom to
play and pray. May the sparks produce a mighty flame
setting off an international conflagration of liberty that all
the forces of tyranny together will be incapable of stopping,
stifling, or smothering.

Even as 1776 so inexorably led to 1976, may America's
freedom lead inevitably to freedom for every
person in this world.
Amen.

Thanksgiving Day

We thank you, Lord, for friends who
continue to be friends even after they
know us well; for people who love us
even after they have seen us at our worst;
for public servants; preachers, teachers,
police officers, firemen, and church workers,
who serve us faithfully even though we never
stop to thank them; for all those who never
stop doing good work just because no one
expresses gratitude.
We thank you today for the brave people
of our land who are more interested in being
right than in being popular; for those who
are willing to support a good cause publicly
even though they know that cause may not
succeed.
We are thankful, Lord, for our freedom—
for the freedom to choose our religion;
for the freedom to choose our profession,
trade, or career; for the freedom to travel
from state to state without passing armed
border guards; and for the freedom to write
letters to the editor, or place an
advertisement in the newspaper, or rent a
hall to speak.
We thank you, Lord, for our human rights—
for the right to vote to elect the men
and women to office who pass the laws of
this land; for the right to vote out
of office those who prove unworthy of
our trust; for the right to elect the
leader of our nation; and for the right

to publicly disagree with him as we choose,
without the fear of a knock at the door
in the black of night, or a wiretap on
our private telephone line.
I am thankful today for all of the medical
miracles we take for granted; insulin,
oxygen, aspirin, eye glasses, pacemakers,
hearing aids, and artificial limbs.
Thank you, Lord, for the doctors who sometimes
rush over slippery highways, through the
dark of night, risking their lives to save
the life of someone whose face they have
never seen and whose name means nothing
to them.
I am thankful for young people who dare
to believe they can improve upon the
achievements of their parents, but truly
appreciate all the older generation has done before them.
I am thankful for older people who dare
to believe that the world can succeed
and improve without them.
I am thankful today for the beauty of
the world around me, for green pastures
and still waters, for tall trees that
bow their heads prayerfully in the wind
and in the sun.
And finally, Lord, I am thankful
for the church that brought the joy
of living into my life when it introduced
me to the person who has become
my best friend—Jesus Christ!
Amen.

A Christmas Prayer

You lead me, Jesus Christ, to thoughts of God.
I see you in a manger carved from a tree.
I see you as a young man with hands that
    reach to touch hearts that hurt.
Your caring reaches out like the strong and
    kind branches of a gentle tree reach out
    to invite road-weary and travel-worn wayfarers
    to quiet rest.
I see you again hanging on a tree with outstretched
    arms taking in the whole world.
From your cross, you show me that God will stop at
    nothing to save my soul.
So, I celebrate God's love today as I celebrate
    your birth around a twinkling Christmas tree.
I pray my life, like yours, O Lord, may be tall
    and upright as a pine tree pointing, reaching,
    sharing, sparkling, life-giving; solid, sturdy,
    strong-rooted in God's love, a beautiful soul,
    evergreen forever.
Amen.

PRAYERS
FOR
TIMES OF
STRESS

When I Am
Weary in Spirit

As an unexpected gust
of wind comes
under the faltering wings of a travel-weary bird
to lift the tired creature to higher altitudes
where it can soar and glide with new strength,
so God, come with an invasion
of unexpected and inspiring ideas
into my mind
to give me the new lift I need.
Thank you, God.
Amen.

When I Face
a Storm in Life

You never promised, Lord, that I would
be forever sheltered from stormy times
in my life. You have promised that the
sun will outlast the storms.
You issue the grand command from outer
space and the renegade storm clouds
break up, scatter, and flee like hoodlums
furtively racing from the streets, back
to their hidden lairs in some forbidding
alley. The bright stars come out to laugh
again, like little children returning
once more to safe streets for happy play.
The sky clears. A huge, yellow moon sails
once more calm and serene through the
silent skies.
Even as you restore peace after the storm,
so will you bestow a renewed calm to my
troubled mind through your peace-instilling
presence that is surrounding me now.
Your quiet and calming spirit is flowing
within me now. My fear is gone!
Thank you, Lord!
Amen.

When It Looks Like
I Have Failed

Lord, are you trying to tell me something?
For—
Failure doesn't mean I'm a failure.
  It does mean I haven't yet succeeded.
Failure doesn't mean I have accomplished nothing.
  It does mean I have learned something.
Failure doesn't mean I have been a fool.
  It does mean I had enough faith to experiment.
Failure doesn't mean I've been disgraced.
  It does mean I dared to try.
Failure doesn't mean I don't have it.
  It does mean I have to do something in a different way.
Failure doesn't mean I am inferior.
  It does mean I am not perfect.
Failure doesn't mean I've wasted my life.
  It does mean I have an excuse to start over again.
Failure doesn't mean I should give up.
  It does mean I must try harder.
Failure doesn't mean I'll never make it.
  It does mean I need more patience.
Failure doesn't mean you have abandoned me.
  It does mean you must have a better idea!
Amen.

To Change My Mood

O God, when a life has been so richly blessed
as mine has been, it is not right for me not
to be laughing! I confess that I am responsible
for my moods. I have no right to selfishly
indulge in negative feelings of self-pity.
It's time for me to change my mental dial,
Lord. You are helping me.
This will be the moment when the sun breaks
through the parted clouds, and the springtime
returns after winter.
Thank you, Lord! The dreary, depressing,
disconsolate mood disappears like
the morning mist in the glowing sunshine of
your love.
And joy moves in!
And hope begins to build up within me!
And a beautiful feeling of love starts to
surround me!
Thank you, God, for the great things you are
doing within me now in this moment of prayer.
Amen.

When I Face My Fears

Turn, O Lord, my fears around.
Let them become a positive force
for good in my life until I—
Fear not that I might fail.
    But fear rather that I might never dare to discover my
      potential.
Fear not that I might be hurt.
    But fear rather that I might never experience growing
      pains.
Fear not that I might love and lose.
    But fear rather that I might never love at all.
Fear not that people may laugh at my mistakes.
    But fear rather that God will say to me "O ye of little
      faith."
Fear not that I might fail if I try again.
    But fear rather that I might miss my greatest chance for
      happiness if I failed to give hope another opportunity.
Amen.

Thanks for Tough Times

Thank you, Father, for rugged friends who care enough
to dare to be rough.

—For the grinding wheel that puts a
fresh edge on the knife;
—for the hoe that breaks up hard soil
and plows out weeds;
—for the sharp knife of the gardener
that prunes and snips useless growth
to give greater strength to the roots
and trunk;
—for the north wind that forces the
pine tree to send down stubborn roots
into granite earth;
—for the rod in the shepherd's hand
that strikes the sheep lest it run blindly
off a precipice;
—for the surgeon's scalpel that cuts
away a foreign tumor;
—for the sculptor's hard hammer and
brutal chisel that chip and polish.
The wheel, the hoe, the knife,
the wind, the rod, the scalpel, the hammer—
these are my rough friends.
So I thank you, God, for the toughening
experiences of life.
It is, I trust, your way
of leading and shaping my life.
I thank you for your tough love!
Amen.

To Face Difficulties

Truly, Father, all things work together
for the good of those who love.
Thank you for the difficulties that produce
divine dividends.
I know that pain is only a phase of the
growing process: that seed buried alive
under suffocating ground in a windowless
grave agonizes before it ruptures into
new life.
I know that I build hard muscles in heart,
mind, and body only when I lift heavy
loads. I thank you for tough times that
produce callouses that could save my
spirit from softness that would be
weakness.
There have been times, O Lord, when
only through great difficulty have I learned
the valuable lessons. I was too blind to
see, too arrogant to believe, or too
stubborn to accept any other way than
by a bed of pain.
I praise you for the times an open door
slammed in my face and forced me out
of an old rut that I never would have
had the courage to leave, and led me down
the road to a beautiful new life.
I thank you for heartbreak which caused
me to bury the hatchet and speak again
to someone I had for far too long been
out of touch.
Thank you, Father, for life's priceless
times of fruitful difficulty.
Amen.

When I Cannot Sleep

O God, around me an unlighted world
huddles in chilly shadows. Will daylight
never come? I wait for the morning calm—
for the morning peace after a night
of unrest.
Now, out of the silent shadows, I wait
for the sweet, fresh, wide-awake note
of a bird, for the awakening birds that
will make the morning happy with music.
The long awaited sunrise is near.
Daylight will soon be restored!
The fitful night will give way to a
new day filled with possibilities!
It's always sunrise, sometime,
somewhere! After every retreating
storm there follows, on golden paths of
sunlight, a returning, refreshing,
renewing peace. After bleak and barren
winter, the springtime always blossoms
with fresh fragrance.
So until the first bird sings,
I will enjoy this quiet moment of
unsleeping solitude.
I shall quietly rest and relax
knowing I am protected from unwelcome
interruptions.
We are alone, together, Lord.
What surprises are you planning
for me tomorrow?
Amen.

For Trying Times

Thank you, Father—

For dangers
that teach me to be brave;
for suffering
from which I learn patience;
for pain
which teaches me tenderness;
for false friends
whose lack of trust
causes me to prize my true friends;
for illness
which teaches me to treasure my health,
a gift I too often take for granted.

Thank you
for leading me through trying times,
without which
I would be like a plant in an overprotected hot house—
too tender
ever to live in the open wind.
Help me to remember
in this trying time
that there is
no progress without pain,
no conversion without crisis,
no birth without painful travail,
no salvation without agonizing repentance,
no Easter without Good Friday,
no service without suffering.

Trying times are times to try
more faith!
I'm trying! You're helping.
Praise the Lord.
Amen.

Praise God for Trouble

For the beautiful blessings of life that
come masquerading as troubles, I thank you,
Lord. I know that trouble is not always
misfortune. It is often your wise way of:
protecting me from an unknown hazard
on the road ahead;
sheltering me from a sin which, unknown
to me, lurks furtively in my path waiting
to trick me or trip me.
Thank you for friendly troubles:
troubles that help me clean up collected
clutter that I have valued too
highly and did not have the courage
to discard;
for troubles that force me to move out
of my life an unworthy friend whom I am
unable to help and who is not a good
influence in my life;
for troubles that make me furious
enough to fight for a good cause that I
foolishly thought I was too busy to serve;
for troubles that frustrate me until I

quit my job that too long has been hiding
my real talents;
for troubles that force me to discover
new skills and abilities that were lying
deep within me, undiscovered, undeveloped,
and undetected, like veins of gold beneath
a cabbage field;
for troubles that cause me to bury the
hatchet and speak once again to an estranged
friend;
for troubles that make me forget myself
and start thinking of others who need me
desperately;
for troubles that turn my greed into
generosity, my hardness into compassion,
my thoughtlessness into consideration,
my cynicism into childlike faith.
Thank you for troubles that really are
not troubles after all, but only blessings
in disguise! I praise you, oh, Lord!
Amen.

For Solutions

Lord,
thanks
for assuring me
that you'll solve the problems
if I'll show the faith
to make the right decision!
Forgive me for waiting
for all difficulties, real and fanciful,
to be resolved
before deciding to make my commitment.
I confess
I have too often allowed problems
instead of possibilities
to take command over my destiny.
I know, now, what faith is, Lord!
It's making the right decisions before I see
solutions to all the problems!
Increase my faith!
Amen.

PRAYERS
IN THE
FACE OF DEATH

When the Road Ahead Is Short

O God, from the vantage point of today
the road ahead looks very short.
I sense that I am about to reach the end.
Remind me that every time of ending
is always a time of new beginning.
Every time one door closes, another door
opens. Every sunset is a move closer to
a new sunrise. Death is always the
prelude to resurrection.
Help me to forgive myself for my
imperfections and faults. I dishonor
you when I disgrace myself by nursing
regrets over my human shortcomings.
Help me to honor you by recalling great
accomplishments you made possible
through my life.
So let me come to the end of the road
with pride behind me, love around me,
and hope ahead of me—only to discover
that what I thought was the end of the
road is a bend in the road leading me into an
exciting new world of opportunity or eternity.
Amen.

At the Death of a Husband or Wife

Thank you, Father, for giving us as much
time together as we had. Spare me
now from further pain of self-pity.
I accept the fact that I have no right to
expect that I can be so highly privileged
as to never taste
sorrow in my lifetime. This is my time
to experience a cross and I do so
bravely.
I remember with joy and eternal gratitude
our wedding day. You made no promise
to us then, guaranteeing a fixed number
of years together. I thank you for what
we have had. And I will not think about
what we could have had.
I will look now at what I have left, not
at what I have lost. I weigh the fruit of our
love and marriage in terms of years
happily spent in our family joys that live
on in happy memories.
I thank you, Father, that our marriage
terminated, not in bitter grief, but

in sweet sorrow. There was no ignoble
scene of angry parting, only the
honored call of God who has glorified
our marriage with the call of eternity:
"Well done, good and faithful servant.
Enter into the joy of your Lord."
My tears are happy tears of love and
gratitude. I thank you that our love
for each other is still alive this
moment.
I sense that I am surrounded by an
invisible presence and power of an
indescribable love. It is the comfort of
your Holy Spirit. I praise you, my God
and my Father, for your goodness and
mercy.
I have tasted grief,
but I will not have wasted this grief.
It shall make me into a softer, gentler soul!
In Jesus' name.
Amen.

At the Death of a Parent

Father, I have so much to be thankful for
today. My father/mother lived long
enough for me to know him/her.
Strengthen me now for the responsibility
that I inherit today. If in your Providence,
I am ever entrusted with a high and
honorable title of parenthood, may I so
live that I may be an unfailing source
of wisdom, security, and encouragement
to my children.
Remove the guilt of my grief today.
From this loss, I find that I could and
should have done more. But I am not
perfect. You know this, and my father/
mother knew this. I thank you for
flooding this moment of my life with
divine forgiveness. You are righting
every wrong and I thank you.
As the fruit of the love of my father and
mother, I shall live on. I dedicate and

commit myself to live honorably and respectfully
so that the remainder of my years brings no
disgrace to my family's name. I rejoice and thank
you for Christ's promise of eternal life.
"He who lives and believes in me shall
never die."
"In my Father's house there are many
mansions."
I am strengthened now by your word:
"When my father and mother forsake me,
then the Lord will take me up."
I know that sorrow never leaves us where
it finds us. I remember it is not what
happens to me in life but how I react to
what happens to me that is supremely
important. Now, God, you will be
constantly my heavenly parent.
"Weeping may endure for the night,
but joy comes in the morning."
Amen.

At the Death of Our Child

Thank you, Father, that our child is not
lost. We know where the child is.
Thank you, Father, that you knew and
loved our child before we did. We believe
you loved and do love our beloved
even more than we do. We can truly,
totally and tenderly entrust this soul to
our eternal, heavenly Father whose
perfect and immortal will has brought
even now an eternal joy to the living
soul of our child.
Thank you for giving us the honor of
sharing in the joy of creating an immortal
soul that shall never die. Heaven is
forever enriched, and our lives are
immeasurably and permanently changed
—because we once held this little life
in our hands and hearts.
We accept the fact, O Lord, that we
can never change what has happened to us,
but we can control how this affects us.
With your strength growing within us,
we shall choose this moment of grief to
become gentle, more compassionate,
more loving, more caring, more Christlike persons.
In Jesus' name.
Amen.

At the Death of Someone Very Young

Thank you, Father. It is not how long
we live that counts, but how beautifully
we live that matters.
Help us to remember that it's the donation
of the life more than duration that adds
eternal significance to a life.
We thank you for the treasured memories
that will forever enrich our lives because
of _____ whom you have called to
live and love with you.
Help us to make our lives more dedicated,
more devoted, that we may through
beautiful living justify in fruitful and
creative labor the longer years you are
giving us.
In the name of our Lord, your only Son,
who was so young himself when he died
on the cross.
Amen.

PRAYERS
FOR
QUALITIES
OF LIFE

For Spiritual Awareness

Too often, O God, the sacred calm of
your still small voice is overpowered by
the roar of the traffic, the moan of
ambulances, the wail of sirens, the growl
of buses, the rude interruption of the
doorbell. Jet airplanes, trucks, trains,
television, telephones fill my everyday
world with noises my ears were never
designed to tolerate.
An irritating assortment of unnatural
sounds drowns your silver-soft voice, Lord,
which whispers through the trees.
Oh, my Lord, there are birds winging
and I do not see them, children playing
and I do not hear them, flowers blooming
and I do not enjoy them, clouds sailing silently
through the soundless sea of space and
I do not see them!
God, you are living and moving and I do
not feel you! Increase my awareness of
the throbbing reality of the dynamic,
spiritual universe around me, Lord.
God! You are moving in mighty thoughts and
feelings within me now! I am surrounded
with an awareness of you that gives me a
new lease on life! Thank you, God.
Amen.

To Feel the Presence of God

As a great wave rises from the deep
to wash away the scratches on the sand,
come, O God, to dissolve forever in
your sea of peace, my cares, my fears,
my worries, and my anxieties.
As the blessed blackness of a quiet night
comes to blanket from my sight the
cluttered collection of billboards,
buildings, and power poles until my eyes
see only bright stars, so come, O God,
and blot out this day's dreary and weary
accumulations of daily irritations, hurts, dents,
and disappointments until I see only
your goodness shining in the shadows.
As an explosion of happy sunshine brings
a joyful glow to dark corners, so come,
O God, and explode your bright joy into
the gloomy corners of my mind.
As a great victorious general awakes
his battalions with a trumpet blast, and

rallies his retreating army with renewing
power, so come, O Lord, and awaken me to
"rise up, be done with lesser things,
to give heart, soul, mind, and strength
to serve the King of Kings."
As the spring rain gently, patiently,
irresistibly falls to soften
the hard crust of frozen ground until it can
receive fruit-producing seed, so, O God,
may showers of your love soak in to soften
the cold corners of my heart, allowing creative
new life to break forth.
As a happy fountain leaps jubilantly and
tumbles joyfully, come, O Holy Spirit, to
transform my melancholy mood until my heart
erupts in joy and happiness.
Oh, Father, make my life a melody like that
of a great wave, a calm night, a morning
sun, a spring rain, a happy fountain!
Amen.

For Peace

Sunshine after rain,
Dewdrops on a rose,
A baby sleeping sweetly in the crib,
A bird drinking from a fountain,
A leaf floating on quiet water, and
A mind focused on God;
Such is the peace I feel
deep within my being
now
as
I close my eyes and think about Jesus Christ.
Thank you, God.
Amen.

For Renewal

Almighty God, it is a beautiful way to
live to know that you are there with
a plan for my life, and through prayer
I can draw my life into harmony with
your plan. I know, God, that your plan
for my life calls for me to follow Christ.
Jesus Christ, I give my life to you.
I've never done it before. That has been
my problem. That has been my hang-up.
O God, I give my life to you now.
Take my life, Jesus Christ, and make it
yours. Forgive my sins. Fill me with
your love. You are doing it now and
I thank you.
Amen.

For Commitment

Today I am making the move.
I am yielding to that positive impulse I've
resisted long enough.

I anticipate problems,
but
I make the commitment
knowing that as soon as I do
powerful forces will come from unexpected sources
to surprise me with their strong support.

I shall not expect perfection
from myself or anyone else.
I am being released
from the bondage of fears,
anxieties, worries, and guilts,
that have
too long
kept me trapped in
indecision and inertia.
I am making that
commitment now.
Thank you, God.
Amen.

For Forgiveness

Yes, I have sinned.
But this does not mean I am a bad person:
It does mean I am a human being.

Praise God!
Christ has forgiven me and I am saved,
for I have accepted Jesus Christ
as my personal Savior.

I now have a beautiful feeling of peace with God.
For God has not only forgiven,
he has forgotten.
He will never bring it up again!
Thank you, Lord.
Amen.

For Grace

I have no right,
Lord,
to ask you to protect me
from all hurts in life.

But do give me the grace
to
turn my scars
into stars.
Amen.

For Confidence

It is flowing into me now,
for my conscience is clear.
I have made the right decision.
I am not afraid of problems.
I will face challenges calmly and serenely
for
God is behind me.
He will help me.
If I must go through difficult times,
he will rescue me.
I feel his spirit of confidence surging in my heart now.

With him I cannot possibly fail.
"If God is for me who can be against me?"
I have a strong feeling
that
everything is going to work out just beautifully.

Thank you, God.
Amen.

For Hope

I have a strong, serene feeling
that
God is planning something good for me today.
I cannot explain it,
but
I have a deep feeling
that wonderful things are in store for me.

I am expecting God to surprise me
with his tender mercy.

He will turn my hurts into halos.
He is guiding my life
in such a way
that whatever happens to me
will prove to be a beautiful blessing.

Thank you, Lord.
Amen.

For Courage

I have it!

My fears are going, going, gone!

I feel a mysterious,
calm,
quiet,
tranquil
assurance rising deep within my being.

This remarkable spirit of courage is overpowering me.

It is the very presence of God
working peace
at the core of my invisible soul.

Thank you, Lord.

All my fears are gone.

What a relief!
Amen.

For Patience

Inch by inch,
Lord,
Anything's a cinch.

Give me more patience,
God.
Amen.

For Perseverance

Deep within myself
I have a powerful awareness that
I have made the right decision
and am moving in the right direction.

I will let nothing and no one
deter, detour, distract, depress, or defeat me.
"No man having put his hand to the plow and
looking back is fit for the kingdom of God."

God's spirit is rising within me
now,
making me very determined
to faithfully keep the beautiful promises
I've made.
I will be faithful.
I am reliable.
Thank you, God.
Amen.

COLLECTED
PRAYERS
OF OTHERS

PRAYERS
FROM
THE BIBLE

Psalmist's Prayer Praising God

O Lord, our Lord, how majestic is thy
name in all the earth! Thou whose glory
above the heavens is chanted by the
mouths of babes and infants, thou hast
founded a bulwark because of thy foes,
to still the enemy and the avenger.
When I look at thy heavens, the work of
thy fingers, the moon and the stars
which thou hast established; what is man
that thou are mindful of him, and the son
of man that thou dost care for him? Yet
thou hast made him little less than God
and dost crown him with glory and honor.
Thou hast given him dominion over the
works of thy hands; thou has put all things
under his feet, all sheep and oxen, and
also the beasts of the field, the birds
of the air, and the fish of the sea,
whatever passes along the paths of the
sea. O Lord, our Lord, how majestic is thy
name in all the earth!

Psalm 8

A Prayer of the Psalmist

Let the words of my mouth and the
meditation of my heart be acceptable in
your sight, O Lord, my strength and
my redeemer.

Psalms 19:14

The Shepherd's Psalm

Because the Lord is my shepherd, I have
everything I need! He lets me rest in
the meadow grass and leads me beside
the quiet streams. He restores my failing
health. He helps me do what honors him
the most.
Even when walking through the dark
valley of death I will not be afraid, for
you are close beside me, guarding,
guiding all the way.
You provide delicious food for me in
the presence of my enemies. You have
welcomed me as your guest; blessings
overflow!
Your goodness and unfailing kindness
shall be with me all of my life, and
afterwards I will live with you forever
in your home.

Psalm 23

David's Prayer

O loving and kind God, have mercy.
Have pity upon me and take away the
awful stain of my transgressions. Oh,
wash me, cleanse me from this guilt.
Let me be pure again. For I admit my
shameful deed—it haunts me day and
night. It is against you and you alone
I sinned and did this terrible thing.
You saw it all, and your sentence against
me is just. But I was born a sinner, yes,
from the moment my mother conceived
me. You deserve honesty from the heart;
yes, utter sincerity and truthfulness.
Oh, give me this wisdom.
Sprinkle me with the cleansing blood
and I shall be clean again. Wash me and
I shall be whiter than snow. And after
you have punished me, give me back my
joy again. Don't keep looking at my sins
—erase them from your sight. Create
in me a new, clean heart, O God, filled
with clean thoughts and right desires.
Don't toss me aside, banished forever
from your presence. Don't take your Holy
Spirit from me. Restore to me again the
joy of your salvation, and make me
willing to obey you. Then I will teach your
ways to other sinners, and they—guilty
like me—will repent and return to you.
Don't sentence me to death. O my God,
you alone can rescue me. Then I will
sing of your forgiveness, for my lips will
be unsealed—oh, how I will praise you.

Psalm 51

The Magnificat: The Prayer of the Virgin Mary

"Oh, how I praise the Lord. How I rejoice
in God my Savior! For he took notice
of his lowly servant girl, and now,
generation after generation forever shall
call me blest of God. For he, the mighty
Holy One, has done great things to me.
His mercy goes on from generation to
generation to all who reverence him.
How powerful is his mighty arm! How he
scatters the proud and haughty ones!
He has torn princes from their thrones and
exalted the lowly. He has satisfied the
hungry hearts and sent the rich away with
empty hands. And how he has helped
his servant Israel! He has not forgotten
his promise to be merciful. For he
promised our fathers—Abraham and his
children—to be merciful to them
forever."

Luke 1:46,55

The Lord's Prayer

And Jesus taught his disciples:
"Our Father which art in heaven,
hallowed be thy name, thy
kingdom come, thy will be done
on earth as it is in heaven.
Give us this day our daily bread
and forgive us our debts as we
forgive our debtors, and lead us
not into temptation but deliver
us from evil, for thine is the
kingdom, the power, and the
glory forever.
Amen.

PRAYERS
OF JESUS

Three Prayers

And Jesus was filled with the joy of the
Holy Spirit. "I praise you, O Father, Lord
of heaven and earth, for hiding these
things from the intellectuals and worldly
wise and for revealing them to those
who are as trusting as little children."

Luke 10:21

And Jesus lifted up his eyes. "Father, I
thank thee that thou hast heard me. And
I knew that thou hearest me always, but
because of the people which stand
by, I said it, that they might believe that
thou hast sent me."

John 11:41, 42

"Now my soul is deeply troubled. Shall
I pray, 'Father, save me from what lies
ahead'? But that is the very reason why I
came! Father, bring glory and honor
to your name."

John 12:27

In Gethsemane

And Jesus fell on his face and prayed,
saying "If it be possible, let this cup pass
from me, nevertheless, not as I will, but
as thou wilt."

And Jesus prayed the second time,
"O my Father, if this cup may not pass
from me, except I drink it, thy will be
done."

And Jesus prayed the third time saying
the same words.

Matt. 26:39-44

On the Cross

Three times Jesus prayed as he died upon the Cross:

"Father, forgive them for they know not what they do."

"My God, my God, why hast thou forsaken me."

"Father, into thy hands I commend my spirit."

Luke 23:24, Matt. 27:46, Luke 23:46

PRAYERS
OF
THE SAINTS

St. Francis of Assisi

Lord, make me an instrument
of thy peace.
Where there is hatred, let me sow love;
where there is injury, pardon;
where there is doubt, faith;
where there is despair, hope;
where there is darkness, light;
where there is sadness, joy.
O Divine Master, grant that I may
not so much seek to be consoled, as to
console; to be understood, as to
understand; to be loved, as to love.
For it is in giving, that we receive;
it is in pardoning, that we are pardoned;
it is in dying, that we are born to
eternal life.
Amen.

Saint Patrick

May the strength of God pilot us.
May the power of God preserve us.
May the wisdom of God instruct us.
May the way of God direct us.

Frank Laubach

Ah, God, what a new nearness this brings
for thee and me, to realize that thou
alone canst understand me, for thou alone
knowest all! Thou art the only being in
the universe who is not partly a stranger!
I invite others inside, but they cannot
come all the way. Thou art all the way
inside with me—here—and every time
I forget and push thee out, thou art
eager to return!
Ah, God, I mean to struggle tonight
and tomorrow as never before, not once
to dismiss thee. For when I lose thee
for an hour, I lose and the world loses
more than we can know. The thing thou
wouldst do can only be done when
thou hast full swing all the time.
Amen.

Zoroaster
(Persian Mystic)*

All that I ought to have thought and have
    not thought;
All that I ought to have said and have
    not said;
All that I ought to have done and have
    not done;
All that I ought not to have thought and
    yet have thought;
All that I ought not to have spoken and
    yet have spoken;
All that I ought not to have done and yet
    have done;
For thoughts, words, and works, I pray
    for forgiveness and repent with
    penance.
Amen.

*The three Wise Men who brought their gifts to the
Babe in the manger were believed to be followers of
Zoroaster.

Brother Laurence

O loving kindness, so old and still so new,
I have been late in loving thee.
O Lord, enlarge the chambers of my
heart that I may find room for thy love.
Sustain by thy power lest the fire of
thy love consume me.
Amen.

Saint Bernardine

O God, acknowledge what is thine in us,
and take away from us all that is not
thine, for thy honor and glory.
Amen.

Saint Augustine

Lord, teach me to know thee,
And to know myself.
Amen.

John Wesley

O Lord, let us not live to be useless.
Amen.

E. Stanley Jones

O Christ, thou art life's supreme
affirmation. I look at thee and anything
becomes possible. I am merging my life
with thy creative life. In thee I too am
creative—we are creative together.
O Christ, thou art adequacy and power.
So I come to thee to get adequacy and
power to live by. I throw open every pore
of my being to let thee come in to
change me from inefficiency to efficiency.
O Christ, I am a part of eternal
significance, eternal plans working
themselves out through me. I can
contribute spirit when I cannot contribute
bigness—and maybe the spirit is the
bigness.
Amen.

An Invitation

Dear Lord, may I humbly invite you to live in my heart, this lovely temple which has served me long and laboriously and which has always struggled to become worthy of you.

Although the door is open wide and the welcome mat is out, there is much housecleaning to be done. It is taking me a lifetime to get it done, so I can't wait until it is completed before asking you in. The corners are full of the dust of disuse, the cobwebs of neglect; the attic is full of broken promises, unwanted responsibilities, hidden desires, forgotten dreams; the basement overflows with the seeds of discontent, the coals of resentment, the tears of sorrow and self-pity; but through the door I feel the light from your face shining, and the assurance of your warm and tender presence gives me fresh hope and courage to face the future.

Won't you come in today?

Amen.

Sara Zimmerman

"HOUR OF POWER" PRAYERS

For Greater Faith

O God, Father of us all, give us a
strong awareness of your presence and
a steady faith in your promises. May our
faith give reality to the things we hope
for; give wings to our hopes and rest to
our fears. Add courage to our faith, so
that by, trusting you, we may dare big
things for you.
Save us from the kind of feeble faith
which makes us victims of anxiety and
fear and makes us ashamed and confused.
Give us a sense of dignity and worth
by sending us some work to do for you;
help us to accomplish something great
for you and your kingdom before we
leave this world.
May the Spirit that was in Jesus so
possess our minds and wills that we may
share his love and purpose and radiant
faith in you.
Hear us, Father, graciously, in this our
prayer offered in Jesus' name.
Amen.

Raymond Beckering

For All Who Work

We pray, our Father, for all who in your world minister in one way or another to the needs of our families and our communities; those who produce our food and make our clothing; those who keep us aware of what is going on in our world through our daily mail, the morning paper, the telephone, or television and radio; and for those who toil away in the sometimes monotonous round of domestic duties in the home. Bless all who make our lives run more smoothly in today's modern and often complicated world. May all these come to realize the dignity and significance of service and to know that any helpful deed done in your name is an act of worship. Help us, in turn, to render some service to another that will make a burden lighter or a pathway brighter. This our prayer is offered in the name of Christ who said, "I am among you as one who serves."
Amen.

Raymond Beckering

For Victory Over Fear

Heavenly Father, you are the guard and
guide of all who place their trust in you.
Give us believing minds and trusting
hearts. You know the cares that often
beset us and torment us. You see the path
that stretches out before us more clearly
than our eyes can discern it. Forgive the
anxieties that cloud our minds and
consume our energies. In you and your
promised word, may we rest and be
strong. Save us, Father, from undue
self-concern, from dark fears, from
distrust in your care. Into your hand of
love, we place our hands, and we face
the future unafraid. So shall your peace,
which passes all understanding, be our
strength and joy. Then each passing
day will bring new proof of your love
and faithfulness. At this moment, we rise to
discover your plan, and this we pray in
the name of him who is the victory,
even Jesus Christ our Lord.
Amen.

Raymond Beckering

To Live
Beyond Ourselves

O God, who asks from us only that we do
justly, love mercy, and walk humbly with
you, help us to live according to your
will.
O Christ, who was rich, yet for our sakes
became poor, that we through your
poverty might become rich, help us with
our riches to enrich the lives of others.
O Savior, who in compassion fed the
multitudes with bread and in mercy
healed the sick, help us like you
to be always understanding and merciful.
O Divine Lord, who welcomed little
children to yourself and rebuked those
who caused them to stumble, help us to
save the children of the world from
hunger and fear, and you, who wiped
tears from the faces of men and women,
help us to bring comfort to the sad.
Father, in your faithfulness, hear this our
prayer and in your graciousness
answer. In Jesus' name.
Amen.

Raymond Beckering

Prayer for Your Tomorrow

May God bless you with
    a clear dawning,
    a cool morning,
    a warm noonday,
    a golden sunset,
    a gentle twilight,
    a starlit night,

and if clouds should cross your sky,
may God give you the faith to look for
the silver lining.
Amen.

AUTHOR